Marketing Mojo

Marketing Mojo

Brand Building in an Age of Consumer Control

*David Herscott
(with Jim Matthews &
Craig Evans)*

iUniverse, Inc.
New York Lincoln Shanghai

Marketing Mojo
Brand Building in an Age of Consumer Control

iUniverse books may be ordered through booksellers or by contacting:

iUniverse
2021 Pine Lake Road, Suite 100
Lincoln, NE 68512
www.iuniverse.com
1-800-Authors (1-800-288-4677)

ISBN-13: 978-0-595-37642-1 (pbk)
ISBN-13: 978-0-595-82033-7 (ebk)
ISBN-10: 0-595-37642-8 (pbk)
ISBN-10: 0-595-82033-6 (ebk)

Printed in the United States of America

Contents

ACKNOWLEDGEMENT

A single page can't fully express my gratitude to the following people for their support in making this book a reality. Nonetheless, it's a start. To each of you, thank you so much.

To Jim Matthews—For your considerable marketing expertise and impassioned coaching.

To Craig Evans—You were instrumental in formulating many of these concepts.

To Colin Ayres—Without you, this book might not be what it might be.

To Rob Gaudio—For sharing the vision and for your patience.

To Mark Albertazzi, Andy Creighton, Alison Swift and Wendy Hutchison—For your insight, ideas and support.

To my wife Dana—When no one else did, you believed. All my love.

FOREWORD

by Nick Wreden

Type in "branding" on Amazon's search engine and thousands of titles will appear. However, most of the books aren't worth reading, even if they wear the mantle of "best-selling." Only politics has more nonsense written about it.

Many of the books on branding are not worth reading for several reasons. The first is that many are nothing more than variations on the same theme: Do more! Do better! Do bigger! It's like the cars in a NASCAR race—all turning left, trying to get bragging rights by reaching the same destination faster than any one else. Other books merely repeat the same ideas you've heard again and again. It's really unfortunate for branding, really. While management, logistics, manufacturing, and financial concepts have advanced dramatically in the last 20 years, branding remains stuck in a back-to-the-future time warp, repeating the ideas—no, clichés, really—that we all learned in Marketing 101.

What management, logistics, and manufacturing have recognized is that the world has changed. Anyone reading this via PDF, while being interrupted by a mobile phone with a friend bragging about his new car, at the same time needing to IM someone about a great restaurant, and monitoring an eBay bid, also understands the world has changed. Because you are so interconnected with your friends and associates, because you can learn more about a product in 60 seconds than a man of the 60's could learn in a month, it is you, the consumer, who has the power now. You have the power to define brands. You have the power to shape them. And, most important, you have the power to determine whether brands live or die.

Unfortunately, many companies raised by the old mantras of the past, like "positioning" or "immutable laws" in an ever-changing world, don't understand that. They think they can use once-powerful tools such as "we-the-leader" positioning or large advertising budgets to get consumers to buy their products. But, it just doesn't work that way anymore. That's why, according to McKinsey & Co. and other leading consulting organizations, up to 95% of all products fail to become brands, even after spending—and wasting—large sums in the process.

So it should be obvious to anyone that it's time for a new approach to branding. It should be one that is accessible to both large and small businesses. It should be one that you don't have to have a Harvard MBA to understand. And, without a doubt, it should be one that works.

Fortunately, David Herscott has given us that approach. *Marketing Mojo: Brand Building in an Age of Consumer Control* first clarifies why the traditional, by-the-college-textbook method common to many agencies just doesn't work any more. Internet. DVDs. Big-screen televisions. iPods. What-ever the pundits claim is the reason, it's obvious to anyone who compares schedules today versus those of a decade ago, that attention is the scarcest resource of all. When the average consumer is exposed to more than 5,000 advertising messages a day, your carefully crafted ad is likely to get all the attention of a grain of sand in a sandstorm.

So what are companies to do in an age where customers not only make the rules but also define the game? The essence of *Marketing Mojo* can be summed up with this insight: Your marketing has to adapt. Stop talking about who your company wants to be and start delivering what customers demand. That's how you earn loyalty.

It doesn't take a lot of money. In fact, *Marketing Mojo* has been crafted for companies with limited time and resources. In the now-dead mass economy, the big-bang approach to marketing might have worked, but in an era of customer control, you need laser-guided smart marketing tools to precisely hone in on—and connect with—the specific customers who can make you a brand. This intelligent marketing is based on four common-sense principles: unification, differentiation, motivation, and communication.

Since marketing budgets are so tight, it is critical to squeeze every ounce of leverage out of every cent. To do this, it is important to understand that "the organization is the brand." As *Marketing Mojo* puts it: "Everything communicates." Every aspect of your organization—from business cards to brochures to packaging—and everyone in your organization must march in lockstep toward the same, unified branding goal, guided by an executive vision based on customer requirements.

You have to say the right thing to the right people. That seems to go without saying. Yet, many companies fail at this because they fail to understand both what customers value and what value they deliver to customers. By walking through the simple, thought-provoking exercises in Marketing Mojo, companies can understand how to get the long-standing attention they deserve from customers who count.

Next, you have to deliver the message. This first requires the operational capabilities to consistently deliver the value customers need. This is especially critical for word-of-mouth marketing, the most powerful tool to leverage your Marketing Mojo. Another critical element is a media plan that answers the "5 Ws" and gets your message across as cost-effectively as possible.

Finally, and most important, you have to measure your efforts. The Internet offers numerous options to track your Marketing Mojo. But your branding effectiveness can also be tracked through a wide variety of options, ranging from the number of on-time shipments to complaints to referrals.

More than one observer has noted that "branding is simple to understand; hard to do." What could be simpler than knowing you must connect to customers as part of a long-term relationship? But executing all the principles in *Marketing Mojo* can not only kick-start your brand to profitable success, but also ensure that the benefits continue to pay off for years to come.

Not bad for a short book of hard-won wisdom.

Nick Wreden (MA, MS) is the CEO of FusionBrand and author of <u>ProfitBrand: How to Increase the Profitability, Accountability and Sustainability of Brands</u> and <u>FusionBranding: How to Build Your Brand for the Future</u>.

1

Why This Book Exists

> 77% of DVR owners do not watch any television advertising.
>
> —*KnowledgeNetworks.com*

Stop me if you've heard this one.

A stranger walks into a bar…I know, bear with me. Inside he finds three gentlemen: an advertising executive, an accountant, and a man holding a bottle of Marketing Mojo.

First, our stranger sits down next to the ad exec, pulls out a one-dollar bill, and slams it down on the bar, "What can you give me for this?"

The ad guy looks down at the dollar bill, then up at the man and replies, "85 cents. Your dollar minus my fee."

The stranger stands up and walks over to the accountant. Once again he slams the dollar down and says, "What can you give me for that?"

With mock sincerity, the accountant replies, "Uh, one dollar…idiot."

Disappointed, the stranger moves on to the third man holding a bottle of Marketing Mojo.

"Well, buddy, how 'bout you, what are you going to give me?" Waving the bill in the air.

Without a word, the man reaches into his pocket, takes out a five-dollar bill and slams it on the bar. Pointing at the interrogator he says, "Only if you're smart about it."

Not that funny, but it's true. The benefit of Marketing Mojo is making every dollar spent on marketing work like five. Yep, it's true, you can spend less and reap more.

The Media Environment—Increasingly Fragmented

Competitive. Complex. Fragmented. This is the marketing landscape your business faces today and will face in the future. Just take a look around. You can't go 10 seconds without being accosted by someone's marketing message. Everywhere you look, another business is trying to compete for your attention and your dollar. Look across your desk, look around your office, look outside, and now look at yourself. Not pretty is it? Yes, even you are a walking billboard. How many logos have you counted? If it's less than ten you probably live in a remote forest somewhere.

Fact is, the average American spends 60 minutes a day listening, reading, and watching a barrage of advertisements (UN Publications, 2003). Not hard to believe since it has been estimated that the average person is subjected to at least 5,000 marketing messages a day and that number is only increasing.

True, all this clutter has sparked the economy. There is no denying that marketing is the single largest contributor to the growth of the free economy. But economic growth is the upside. The downside is that the clutter has made consumer time an invaluable resource, almost as much as the almighty dollar. All these messages are vying for time, and unfortunately, that means exponentially more messages barging their way into the consumer's day trying to win that few extra seconds of attention.

What makes it even more difficult is that the consumer is busier than ever. According to a survey by LibrarySpot.com, the average workweek is 46 hours long, 3 hours longer than in the 70's. That means, added up, the average American is working almost four extra weeks a year. A whole month! So, consumers really don't have time to look at marketing messages, even if they want to.

The reality is, the more a consumer sees, the less they trust a message because they can honestly say they have seen everything. Their distrust has become so fervent that they don't even believe actual facts when they hear them. More than 50% of Americans that were surveyed didn't trust news broadcasts (The Pew Research Center, 2004). The news! If they don't even believe the reports on *60 Minutes*, why would they trust your marketing message?

Advertisers must reevaluate their marketing and media choices—if for no other reason than extreme media fragmentation. Until 1995, a radio or television advertisement was the most effective way to reach a consumer. In the early 80's, most households had a television (most without a remote control) and a radio (many with a large antennae). These mediums were the most effective on the planet in positioning brands, because they could deliver a message repeatedly to an audience that was all-eyes and all-ears.

The Age of Consumer Control

Around 1995 came commercial Internet and the end of mass marketing as we knew it. It was the first time in two decades that the attention of audiences was taken away from radio and television and refocused on a brand new one: the computer. What ensued was a dot-com explosion accompanied by a huge influx of advertising, marketing of all kinds, all of the time. But, what made this new medium especially unique was consumer control. Nick Wreden notes in his *FusionBrand* blog that users can now conduct more personal product research and begin to understand just how valuable consumers are as customers. By the turn of the millennium, with eyes and ears on the Internet, it was clear that consumers were gaining total control of how they were exposed to, and interacted with, brands. It meant only viewing products and services they wanted, and avoiding sites with products they didn't.

In the past few years there has been a total coup. Consumer control has increased with innovations such as digital video recorders and satellite radio. Technology like this has made traditional commercials easy to dodge, and has reshaped marketing. Television watchers can now record their favorite shows and fast forward through commercials, stopping only if they see a product they are genuinely interested in. Satellite radio subscribers aren't bothered with commercials at all. A steady stream of their favorite music has replaced the usual format of songs interrupted regularly by commercials. Today, consumers in industrialized nations have almost complete control: the ability to select only the advertising they wish to see or hear, if they wish to at all.

So while consumers are surrounded by an overwhelming amount of marketing clutter, they also have the power to regulate it—it's an On-Demand World. The moment consumers don't need you, you're TIVO'd. Problem is, in order for your company to succeed, you need your audience to listen. So, how do you get their attention? Tell them something they want to hear. Open up the boardroom doors, listen to what the consumer is screaming for, and shape your marketing message around those demands.

Burger King is a perfect example of a brand meeting consumer demand. Their tagline alone, "Have it your way", exemplifies how a company can survive, marketing a product the "consumer's way." Your company should do the same. If you're talking at consumers, stop. Stop talking about who your company wants to be and start delivering what customers demand. That's how you earn loyalty.

Fortunately, it's possible (actually it's slightly ironic too). Mediums like the Internet allow businesses to track, measure, and analyze what audiences are looking for. So, in the midst of increased consumer control, your business can maintain a helpful amount of its own. It's possible to collect and leverage mass amounts of data to understand what your customers are looking for, when they want it, and how they want to get their hands on it.

If utilized properly, these mediums also allow businesses to communicate with the consumer with ease. However, it isn't necessary for a company to be everything to everyone. It's impossible to cater to every individual customer and it's still foolhardy to stand for a number of different things with no focus. Your company should stand for a singular…something. The point is, once you decide who your company is and what service it provides, avoid using repetitive, impersonal messaging to sell. Don't just talk at consumers. Talk with consumers. The bottom line is that consumers buy brands. So no matter how effectively you interact with your customers, make sure they know who you are.

Now, to do that, you must utilize as many mediums as possible. That way you can respond to specific customer needs by tailoring messages and products, and satisfying the target. It isn't about reaching the masses anymore. It's about reaching the right people, at the right time, with the right message. Sure, that means you're totally accountable on all levels of a marketing relationship. But, being Mojofied means establishing a brand that is communicated the right way, so you never have to worry about getting it wrong.

Dominating Your Marketing Arena

So, how can you raise your voice above all that shouting? How do you stand up and say, "Look at me world. I'm different. I'm better. You can trust me and, therefore, you should buy me"? And, how do you do it when your marketing dollar today is worth less than it was thirty years ago? Actually, how do you do it when your marketing dollar is worth less than it was yesterday?

That's what this book is about. By putting in a dollar, you can get five dollars worth of impact. Just to be clear, that's not five dollars in return. The return would be even larger because your budget is acting five times larger than it really is. It's five dollars worth of *impact*. Using one dollar as efficiently and effectively as possible through simple techniques, any company, anywhere can develop Marketing Mojo.

There are businesses out there right now that already have Marketing Mojo. You know who they are: Nike, Target, Starbucks, and Coca-Cola. These are the Titans in their arena. They have a presence that is instantly recognizable and approachable. Wall Street and publications want to cover them, people want to work for them, and their employees get their logo tattooed on themselves. These companies have a certain something—a certain je ne sais quoi.

Yes, these companies spend enormous amounts on marketing each year. They have the resources. But size has nothing to do with Marketing Mojo. These examples are just the most familiar. There are a dozen other companies, which you may not have heard of, that have it "all together." In reality, you probably already know a few, that may be in the same industry as you. These are the companies with the packed trade show booth, the companies that have publications calling to write stories on them, and the companies that have sales move on a steady pace.

Stop fooling yourself by thinking, "Well, they have the budget. I don't." It isn't about that. There will always be companies outspending yours. The catch is that the money spent on marketing is only worthwhile if the money is effective. In other words, rather than outspending, try to "out Mojo" your competition. Consider this: say your company is the same size as Nike. If you and Nike each had a million dollars to spend on marketing, which do you think would yield a better return? That's what Marketing Mojo is all about: "out marketing" your competition.

The Importance of Marketing

Now, hopefully, your company aspires to be the next Nike or Coca-Cola, but few organizations have the time, resources, or insight to do what it takes to stake out real estate on the mental maps of their key audiences. Product cycles shorten, budgets tighten, competition grows, and marketing messages flood the audience's senses. It is now more important than ever to make every dollar work like five.

Few companies are willing to put forth the time, energy, and brainpower to create an effective marketing program that is resilient and recognizable. But while you may not need your product to become a household name, it is important for your customers, your vendors, and your employees to recognize, respect, and most of all prefer you.

The most important endeavor a company can undertake is marketing. Companies have made skyscraping piles of money through effective marketing, and most without unusual, special, or wonderful products. Do you think that cup of coffee was worth four bucks? Do you think that moisturizing lotion was worth four times the generic brand? That friends, is the power of marketing your business.

A Personal Marketing Perspective

One of the nice things about working in the Marketing Communications industry is that you rarely do the same thing twice. You're always looking for a new solution or a new strategy to get your client noticed because their needs are always in flux and marketing objectives evolve from season to season and product to product. As a result, new ideas and executions are always in demand. Furthermore, because marketing communications firms have new clients from year to year, there are always new sets of marketing challenges waiting for unique solutions.

All that makes for an interesting show that I experience first hand every day. From season to season and product to product, I see companies make mistakes over and over again in their marketing efforts.

Our firm is an eclectic group of people from all over the world. Most of them have worked in advertising, marketing or public relations in one form or another, and most in various sized agencies. We've worked on accounts ranging from Fortune 500 Businesses, to tongue scrapers, to the infamous Wendy's "Where's the Beef" campaign. Collectively, we have over 5,000 accounts under our belts. So, we may not have seen it all, but we've seen a hell of a lot.

A commonality among the businesses that we've worked with is that most of them get much bigger bang for their buck. Some of our clients have seen a ten-to-one return on every dollar they invested. Unfortunately, I've heard of other businesses spending a dollar on marketing and then having to spend two more to correct a mistake. To that end, this book is partially based on a collection of insights and research of clients we've worked with and observations of some companies we haven't. The view from here is that, if done properly, companies can maximize the impact of their marketing spending.

There are thousands of other books that offer discourses on essential marketing knowledge and how it's evolving. But I won't assume what those books do. Marketing Mojo is based on the fact that you have:

1.   Limited time

2.   Limited resources

In the following pages, we won't rehash the insights and information provided by the other books. Though, we will poke a few holes in them along the way.

Marketing Mojo is not rocket science. But it isn't falling down either. It requires you to roll up your sleeves, but not empty your wallet. It may take you a couple of hours to read, but this book may save you money, time, and headaches in the future.

2

What is Marketing Mojo?

> In the past 20 years, network share has dropped from 91% to 45%.
>
> —*InsidePolitics.org*

Examples of Mojo

What does it mean to have Marketing Mojo? Look no further than Harley-Davidson Motorcycles for an explanation. This is a company that has managed to create a "rock star" brand, with the kind of attitude that makes doctors and lawyers get the orange and black logo tattooed on their bodies. They continue to sell motorcycles because they effectively market to consumers like these, who want to identify with the brand—the look of Hell's Angels and the feel of adventure on the open road.

Message: Marketing Mojo is a powerful influencer.

The best example is the company that took the place of Woolworth's: Target, now a surprisingly hip brand that was hardly recognizable a few years ago. At the time of this writing, Target is kicking ass and taking names. Literally. And, K-Mart is taking the biggest blows to the face and body. They failed to create any kind of personality and subjected their consumers to confusing messages about who they wanted to be.

Message: Marketing Mojo makes the competition emulate you.

Here's a slightly different example. Have you noticed that in recent years, companies have been striving to develop a little personality and style of their own? Take a look at Apple, W Hotels, Volkswagen, and Mini Cooper. Each has crafted its own distinct, cohesive style that is easily identifiable and approachable for consumers.

Message: Marketing Mojo means setting yourself way apart.

In 1999, Unilever filled headlines when they bought Ben and Jerry's for 24 times it's operating income. Not so preposterous since they believed in Ben and Jerry's strategic business plan and marketing communications.

Message: Marketing Mojo makes sense. And creates value for companies.

Then there's the JABRA Corporation, one of our clients, which makes hands-free communication devices for mobile phones. When you see people walking around apparently talking to no one, it's often a Jabra device they're using. Due to the nature of their business, JABRA is part of the behemoth consumer category that is (insert echo effect here) "wireless communications." As a result, JABRA has to appear at an enormity of trade shows, competing for attention with the likes of Ericsson, Nokia, Sprint, et al.

However, JABRA spent about one-fifth as much as it seems to develop a grander voice, in an already clamoring industry. How? By crafting a visual and messaging identity that could not possibly be missed at the wireless industries' largest trade shows.

But, it is much more than brand identity working in JABRA's favor. When California and New York began talking about legislation to mandate the use of hands-free mobile devices, guess whose photo appeared on the cover of daily newspapers all across those states…Want a hint? It begins with J and ends in ABRA.

Message: Marketing Mojo is effective, especially when working overtime

Defining Marketing Mojo

Your company does not have to be young, hip and socially conscious to have Marketing Mojo. Your company might only be familiar to 1 or 2% of the general consumer population. Statistically speaking, you're probably a B-2-B enterprise. And in that case, it may not be your number one priority for teenagers to want to be associated with you. Either way, you do have customers. Whether they are 18-year-old high school seniors or 48-year-old IT managers, your audience needs to recognize you and make positive associations with you.

So, what is Marketing Mojo? (Drum roll please...) It is the ability to inject and harmonize all facets of your company's communications with a highly charged stimulus to maximize the impact of your marketing dollar.

The net result allows you to get more with less. Implementing a highly charged stimulus of Marketing Mojo should automatically exude the right message to the right people at the right time, thereby eliminating much of the effort that usually goes into marketing.

The Foundation of Marketing Mojo

Marketing Mojo's foundation is supported by four pillars:

1. Unification

2. Differentiation

3. Motivation

4. Communication

Unification. One of the most important aspects of a successful company is to work as one unit and not as a group of small companies.

This is often the case within larger corporations. As companies grow larger, it becomes increasingly difficult to remain unified. The left hand doesn't know what the right hand is doing, and other appendages become increasingly estranged.

The result is what seems like a group of small companies moving in a variety of directions.

Worry not. By telling your employees where you are headed and how you are heading there, Marketing Mojo will have everyone marching in line and to the same drum. This is not a mission statement. Think of it as a Mission Statement on steroids. It provides greater meaning to your employees and gives anyone outside your company walls confidence and security with the familiarity of dealing with a well-defined company. In turn, it makes doing business with your employees and your customers much easier.

In today's market, effective unification means making everyday choices for consumers, like paper towels, easier, and riskier purchases, like a new car, simpler.

Differentiation. Marketing Mojo seeks to find a unique space that your company can call its own. Your employees must have a sense of the difference between themselves and the company around the corner. In other words, what makes your company a special environment? If you are a "me too" company, you can only expect that quality of work from your employees.

Differentiation is a paramount part of marketing. It is literally half the battle. If you feel, look and act like everyone else, why should anyone take notice of you? With so many companies vying for consumers' time, and consumers inevitably tuning out, no one will.

When an organization sets itself way apart it can provide emotional benefits to its customers, vendors, and employees—like Nordstrom's (service) and Saturn (value).

Motivation. The sum of unification and differentiation is motivation. By creating both, Marketing Mojo stimulates the interest of employees, vendors, and customers in your organization. They will know who you are. They will know what you are about. And they will insist they are missing out on it.

Communication. This pillar is essential because everything communicates. Absolutely everything: from business cards to billboards; stationary to employees. Anything associated with your company has something to say. The questions are: What are they saying? Are they all preaching the same thing? And are they presenting the right message, both positively and strategically?

Some Real Results of Marketing Mojo

It increases marketing efficiencies. If your company is well defined, you'll end up spending less to market it.

It increases value among consumers and investors. A Mojofied company will inevitably be able to charge a premium for their products or services. For instance, that $4 cup of Starbuck's coffee you or the person sitting next to you is drinking.

It strengthens resilience. Mojofied companies are able to withstand greater economic turmoil because of public familiarity.

It helps employees excel at their jobs. Removing guesswork about a company's goals allows employees to understand what they are working for and to concentrate on achieving those goals. So instead of putting out small fires everyday, employees will be putting forth a clear, motivated effort.

It makes product and service development easier. A company with a clear strategic direction can develop products and services more easily. For instance, quickly eliminating ideas that don't fit within the strategic constructs.

Lastly, it increases value among investors. Certainly, Nike or Coca-Cola would sell for much more than their market value. Remember the Leveraged-Buy-Out '80's? RJR did not buy Nabisco, they bought Oreo!

What Kind of Business Can Benefit From Marketing Mojo?

With a little Marketing Mojo or a truckload of it, most companies, for-and non-profit, can benefit a great deal. Running a business, marketing aside, is difficult enough. It is a little surprising how few companies view marketing as a fundamental part of their business strategy. Just look at the first budget that is cut when times get tough. It's the marketing budget. Strange, considering it's like a crew team putting down their oars to save energy—makes for a bad race.

But what if you keep rowing, and do it more efficiently? You can get more impact for your marketing dollar because Marketing Mojo stretches your budget and allows you to work less on marketing your organization because of the efficiencies it creates. This way, with each crew member rowing in the same direction at a steady pace, some of the rowers can even stop rowing.

Today is a Great Day to Rethink Your Marketing

Right now there is someone, somewhere out-marketing you. Unless you are one of the aforementioned companies that have stockpiles of Marketing Mojo in warehouses, your marketing dollar isn't working as hard as it could be. And that competition, it isn't going anywhere. Your customers will constantly be swayed by your competitor's messages. They want your customers. And in today's marketing arena, with so many choices for customers, it is becoming increasingly more expensive to reach and keep them.

3

How Mojofied is Your Company?

In 2003, DVR sales topped 2.3 million. By
2009, they'll reach 45.5 million.

—BusinessWeek.com

The Mojo Scale

Want to find out where you are on the Mojo scale? Below is
the Mojofication Quiz, designed to help you figure out where
your business stands next to other Mojofied companies, by
identifying what is and isn't being done effectively. Fact is,
before the "how to," comes the "what to do."

With a good sense of how much Mojofying your business
needs, you can target specific areas that need improvement
and spend more time on them. But, that doesn't mean you
should skip over any remaining part of this book; after all

Marketing Mojo is all about harmonization. But, your company may not need a complete retooling either. The Mojofication Quiz allows you to determine exactly what you need and where you need it. At the end of the quiz, compile your score and see where you stand on the Mojo scale.

Now, it's no easy task to look at your own business and admit that it needs help. But, the point of this quiz is to uncover those areas that need improvement. So, be honest and critical.

The Mojofication Quiz

Part one: Your Brand. For each of the following questions, rate and circle the level of "agreement" based on your current company branding from one to five, five being the strongest. At the end of part one, add up your score and write it on the total line.

Your company has a powerful tagline	Strongly Disagree 1	2	3	4	Strongly Agree 5
Consumers can instantly recognize your brand	Strongly Disagree 1	2	3	4	Strongly Agree 5
Company communications are consistent (e.g., letterhead)	Strongly Disagree 1	2	3	4	Strongly Agree 5

Employees understand where your company stands	Strongly Disagree 1	2	3	4	Strongly Agree 5
Employees believe in where the company is headed	Strongly Disagree 1	2	3	4	Strongly Agree 5
All customers perceive your company the way you want	Strongly Disagree 1	2	3	4	Strongly Agree 5
Employees speak positively about the company	Strongly Disagree 1	2	3	4	Strongly Agree 5

Total: _____

Now it's time for part two: Your Marketing. If any of the following statements are true about your business, circle true. If not, circle false. And, for every answer that's true, give yourself a point. Then add up your points when you're finished with this section and write the total on the line.

You've done a company communications audit in the past year

True   False

You've written and published a book

True   False

Your company does marketing campaigns (e.g. print)

True   False

Your company's website receives
hundreds of unique visitors per day

True   False

You track your website's activity

True   False

You schedule speaking engagements

True   False

You write for online and offline
publications

True   False

Upper management meets fre-
quently with employees

True   False

You've never cut your marketing budget to decrease overhead | True False

You only have one logo | True False

Total: _____

Finally, part three: Your Communication. This is about analyzing your business relationships (a huge part of being Mojofied). Rate and circle each as poor (zero points), fair (one point) or excellent (three points) and record the total.

Vendors | Poor Fair Excellent

Partners | Poor Fair Excellent

Valued/most frequent customers | Poor Fair Excellent

New customers | Poor Fair Excellent

Total: _____

The Results

Now get the sum of all three totals. This grand total will help you figure out how Mojofied your company is.

With a score above 55: Your company is totally Mojofied (or very close to it) and you might want to think about lining a bird cage with the remaining pages of this book rather than reading them. Seriously, if you've already injected all these techniques into your business, you probably need moneybags more than you need advice on effective marketing techniques. In fact, breeze through this book and see if anything important is missing.

With a score between 35 and 55: Your company is mid-Mojo. Refer back to the test; any question that you didn't record as a perfect score can be improved upon. Adopting certain marketing techniques covered in this book can help push your business onto an even higher pedestal. Want to join the elite? Read on.

With a score less than 35: Your company is Mojo-deprived. Not to worry though; you're among the majority; and already way ahead of the curve on remedying things. Using the marketing techniques described in the following chapters, you'll be able to inject Mojo into your business and turn your company into a well-oiled, money-making machine. So, are you ready to get your Marketing Mojo workin'?

4

The Importance of Branding

The percentage of US homes tuned in to the three Big Broadcast Networks (i.e. ABC, CBS and NBC) has dropped from 55% to just over 20% since 1970.

—*Medialit.edu*

It's not that every company should "do branding"; it's just impossible as a company, not to brand.

What Branding Doesn't Mean

The problem with saying "We don't brand" is a semantic one. "Branding" is commonly misperceived. Several years ago, during the Dot Com halcyon days, everyone wanted to do a branding campaign, even though few marketing managers knew what it meant. (You know what happened.)

Today, post Dot Com debacle, the push to "brand" has subsided because those managers have now determined that "branding doesn't work." Ironically, the Dot Com bomb proved just the opposite—branding does work. It's just that no amount of branding will sell stuff to consumers that they don't need or want. Remember, consumers have control.

But, guess what? Every business today is doing a branding campaign, whether they know it or not, because everything a company does is communicating and positioning to the rest of the world: commercials, salespeople, business cards, delivery vans, how the receptionist answers the phone.

Unfortunately, there are about as many definitions of the word "branding" as there are books on the subject. Many companies today—marketing, service, manufacturing, and advertising alike—banter the word around loosely and improperly. There is even disagreement among professionals about this enigmatic word. Asking people to define it is similar to asking them to define irony: "Um, I'm not really sure, but I know it when I see it."

First, here's what branding is NOT:

- A product or line of products

- A logo

- An image advertising campaign

- A weekend employee retreat

- What you think you are

The following examples are a couple of popular definitions. The discrepancy is obvious and the confusion is even clearer.

> A brand is a name.—Joe Marconi, *The Brand Marketing Book*

> A brand is a distinguishing name and/or symbol (such as a logo, trademark, or package design) intended to identify the goods or services of either one seller or a group of sellers, and to differentiate those goods or services from those competitors.—David Aaker, *Managing Brand Equity*

Gasp.

These two definitions represent the branding extremes. One is so vague and the other so specific that both seem to defy any real value. They lack an essential part of the branding equation: people. Therefore, each has a company-centric view of branding.

What Branding Actually Means

First, a company cannot exist without customers. So if branding doesn't revolve around them, the company stops spinning and falls on its side.

The world, particularly the U.S., has become a "service economy," which means service industries tailor goods and services to what consumers want. Forcing new products into the lives of consumers is a thing of the past. So, if you cater to consumer's needs, shouldn't your definition of branding include them? Focusing on the consumer rather than the company, you can create a definition of a brand that is paramount to the way a brand should be considered.

Second, a brand is not a singular idea. It is much more. You cannot point to one aspect of your company, like the name, logo or chief product, and say that's your brand. A brand is a collection of attributes within your entire organization. In other words, it is a sum of all parts.

Finally, you cannot assess your own brand. Scientists believe that an experimenter's results are always slightly altered by the impact of an observer. Similarly, observing, judging, and assessing your brand from the inside out can lead to myopic and flawed thinking and behavior.

Therefore, a brand is not what you say you are. A brand is what everyone else thinks you are. That's what you and your Mojo will manage.

Everything Communicates

Looking at branding from a different angle, it's like a person's personality. Everything a particular individual does—what they say, how they act, the music they listen to, and the type of work they produce—influences how other people think about them. Collectively, these attributes make up a personality. For a company, it's called a brand, and neither a personality nor brand is correctly described or categorized by that person or company, but rather by the people that surround it.

Like a personality, a brand is communicated through every aspect of the company—how the ads feel, how the phone is answered, what the business cards look like. Everything communicates is "pillar four". (More on this later.)

Maintaining an external focus on a branding definition forces companies to focus on the current marketplace. A common problem is that companies creating a brand personality do not adapt to the fluctuating market conditions. While a brand should not change dramatically over time, it should be flexible.

Branding Happens

Brands are defined by what others think about your company. So, inevitably, they create themselves. Even an unguided, strategy-lacking company will develop a brand. But these are hit or miss brands—like derelict ships pushed back and forth by a capricious economic climate. These companies survive for a time floating with the current, but most eventually end up lost at sea. A strong company with a strong brand has a rudder, steering wheel, map, and a compass. These companies have a destination and use the economic climate to their advantage.

According to The McKinsley Quarterly, 1999 #2, "Research into the connection between brand strength and corporate performance at 130 consumer companies suggests strong brands generate, on average, a total return to shareholders that are 1.9% above the industry average, while weaker brands lag behind the average by 3.1%"

Innumerable books have been written on the subject of branding, too. But there's a very good reason. Branding is an essential element of Marketing Mojo.

5

How to Establish Your Mojo

Jonathan Miller, the head of AOL, reported that 60-70% of the time spent on his service is spent with content created by his audience.

—Mobile-Weblog.com

Objectives vs. Strategy

Much like the word branding, these terms are often misused. An objective is something you are trying to achieve. Objectives usually contain or begin with the word "to" and usually look like the following: "Our objective is to sell 1 million units." A strategy, on the other hand, is how you plan to reach an objective. Strategies usually look like this: "We'll sell 1 million units by asking all our acquaintances to buy 10 each."

The Road to Unity

Is Marketing Mojo really about fixing your brand? Yes and no. Mojofying your brand will do two things: improve your corporate strategy and strengthen your marketing. In fact, if implemented correctly, these two aspects run over and affect the rest of your business.

Marketing Mojo's first pillar is about achieving comprehensive unity and direction for your company that is easily followed by the various disciplines within it. Think of it as charting a roadmap that guides you and your employees in thinking. How does that happen? Strategy. Strategy is the most effective way to achieve unity.

In the 1990's there were two schools of thought when it came to running a business. The first was "give it personality." The second was "just do it." Back then, strategies were put in the back seat, while moving products to the market rode in the front—absolute necessities.

Companies didn't want a plan. They wanted personality. The fallacy behind this thinking was evident in the maelstrom of business failure in the early years of the new millennium. For these companies, a little strategic thinking could have created some awareness about the problems of selling a bag of dog food for $10 when it cost $20 to ship it.

Sine then, the pace of the business environment hasn't slowed down at all. Yes, the energy spent trying to surface as a business is now spent trying to stay afloat. But, the competition is just as fierce. The pressure is still there.

> There is the slightly odd notion in business today that things are moving so fast that strategy becomes an obsolete idea. That all you need is to be flexible or adaptable. Or, as the current vocabulary goes, 'agile.' This is a mistake. You cannot substitute agility for strategy. If you do not develop a strategy of your own, you become part of someone else's strategy. You, in fact, become reactive to external circumstances. The absence of strategy is fine if you don't care where you are going.—Futurist Alvin Toffler

Goals and Objectives

So, in the interest of good strategy, you should begin at the beginning.

The first step of the Mojofication process begins with developing that all-important strategy. That starts with a little, if not a truck load of, self-examination. While this may seem painfully obvious, people can learn a lot during this kind of introspection. Do not underestimate the power of realizing, and then knowing, who you are. First there is unification, pillar one; then growth.

So, sit down, put your thinking cap on and ask yourself this question:

What does my company do?

Stop reading and think about it for a second.

Was your answer something like this: "We make wireless phones," or "My company produces confetti"?

This is a bit of a trick question, designed to show you the fallacy of thinking that many marketers fall into. Marketing Mojo begins with the simple knowledge that you are not what you make. The problem with a majority of company's marketing direction is that it is based on what they make and not what they actually do. What's the difference? What you make is merely a byproduct of what you do. In other words, what you do is the guiding principle upon which all other endeavors and activities can be based.

In the examples above, the more accurate responses would have been: "We help people communicate," or "We enhance the fun of celebrating." These answers are the root of a company's experience and the springboard from which new products arise. If your company just makes confetti, how many types of confetti can you make? But, if your company enhances the experience of celebrating, then the gateway to new products and services is widened. In addition, you won't be led away from your core competency.

Isn't this just focusing on the benefits rather than the features? Yes. But you'd be surprised how many companies think their selling point is the products they offer and not the benefits those products provide.

The importance of strategy is further supported by the exclamations of a venture capitalist from the '80's. His frustration was that so few of the business plans he received soliciting investment capital spent much, if any, time outlining a marketing strategy. They were all about the product invention or more often the inventors themselves—the brilliance of the features and the minds that created them. He couldn't have cared less! He was about making money on his investments (a blinding glimpse of the obvious) and therefore only cared that there might be people who wanted the product and would be willing to pay for it. He said one day, "I don't care if these guys make dog crap in a paper bag! Show me that millions of people want it and I'll fund the company." Telling.

That's just for product-oriented companies, though. What about companies that provide services? Well, your response to the earlier question may have been a little closer to the truth. But, it may not have been close enough. For instance, if you're in the travel business, your answer may have been: "We help people find low-cost airfare and travel accommodations." True as that is, on a deeper level you: "Help people escape the speed of life and reinvigorate their souls." With that sort of thinking, how much more could your company do for customers?

Defining Your Organization

Now that you know what your company does and what it means to customers, it's time to wrap it in some defining parameters, or pillar two: differentiation. This will help you delve deeper into what your company is, narrow the focus, and make your marketing even more precise.

You're working your way to the Mojo Mantra, half of pillar three: motivation. The Mojo Mantra is the one thing that you want your employees, customers and potential customers to know about the company. Note that this is one thing, not a variety of things. Whether you make one product or two hundred, to forge a bond between your organization and the people surrounding it, customers and employees alike, there must be one, single, sole, solitary, individual, lone, exclusive idea to believe in.

Chances are that your company has a number of great traits that make it special. It's like a person. No one quality makes a person appealing; it's usually a variety of qualities. Your company is no different. It's valuable because there is a long list of valuable traits. The best way to consolidate them and create a Mojo Mantra is to lead up to it. Start at the very broad, defining characteristics and then begin to narrow them down.

First, the Core Values. These are adjectives, no less than three and no more than five that define what's great about your company. You've already started to define what sets your company apart; now put those ideas into words. These adjectives may not be completely unique. Some may even contradict each other. That's okay. This is intended to take a broad snapshot of your organization that you can whittle down. Don't just concentrate on the adjectives that describe your company in its current state. The point of Marketing Mojo is to move your company in a clear, defining, and motivating direction.

One of the best ways to define yourself is to talk to your current customers. Ask them what they love about you. These are more than likely your strengths, or, Core Values. If your customers tell you that there isn't anything, ask them what you could work on. Those suggestions are the Core Values you can work on. No company is perfect; it's okay if your words are aspiring.

> Your most unhappy customers are your greatest source of learning.—Bill Gates, *Business @ the Speed of Thought*

Think about every single aspect of your company, not just what you're working on today. For example, if you've been in business a while, that's a Core Value. You're *wise*. Or, maybe you haven't been in business very long. You're *scrappy*. You're trying to set yourself apart, so use adjectives to accomplish that.

If you're stuck, here's a list to inspire you.

Bold
Leading
Meticulous
Accessible
Passionate
Experienced
Contemporary
Fun
Innovative
Inspired
Established
Trustworthy
Hip
Intuitive
Family oriented
Passionate
Hungry

Responsive
Friendly
Serious

That's just twenty of thousands of possibilities. What have you come up with?

_____

_____

_____

_____

_____

Getting to the Core

More on pillar two, it's time to decide what your Core Differentiator is—your company's raison d'etre; the one thing that makes your company, your company. What truly sets you apart from the rest of the competition? If you pitched your company in an elevator ride, what would you say on the ride up that makes it stand out?

Using your Core Values, focus on the service you provide. No, not just that you make a great widget. Think about the widget and then put it in terms that are unique to your organization. Here's a tip: do it without using words that say exactly what you make. It's more appealing that way.

For example, if you are a computer hardware manufacturer, your Core Differentiator may be:

We design productivity tools that are visually arresting and surprisingly easy to use.

Now it's your turn.

Fill in the blank. My Company's Core Differentiator is _____

_____

_____

_____

_____

_____

Ready to move on? Now, what role does your differentiator plays in people's lives. What is the Core Benefit that your customers derive from the product or service you offer? Again, there is a powerful emphasis on what your company means to customers, and less on what you actually make. Essentially, you are trying to decide what consumer needs you fulfill.

Using the example above, a computer hardware manufacturer's Core Benefit might be the following:

We make it easier for people to be more productive.

Your turn again.

Fill in the blank. My Company's Core Benefit is _____

_____

_____

_____

_____

_____

The Mojo Formula

With the Core Differentiator and Core Benefit established, you are well on your way to making your marketing more efficient and effective.

The next step is to combine the two into what's called the Mojo Mantra. The Mantra helps provide your team with direction that helps everyone march to the same beat of the same drum. It helps keep your customers in mind and gives you a yardstick to measure new products and ideas.

So, that's: Core Differentiator + Core Benefit = Mojo Mantra

Simply rewrite your Differentiator and Benefit into a grammatically correct statement that flows. Something like this:

"We create visually arresting and surprisingly easy-to-use products that help people increase their productivity."

Fill in the blank. My Company's Mojo Mantra is _____

_____

_____

_____

_____

_____

This is not a mission statement. It could be. But, most mission statements are more like mission paragraphs that incorporate broader, non-marketing notions of the well-being of employees, a system of rewards, history of the company, etc. Mission statements can get so over saturated that they lack a clearly defined marketing proposition. Even if they happen to include a marketing proposition, it is often too grandiose or vague for anyone to understand and to take action.

Does the beginning of this mission statement sound familiar: "(insert company name here) is dedicated to making the world's finest (insert product here)"?

There is nothing wrong with wanting to make the world's finest products or offer the world's finest services. In fact, making the world's finest anything is unique. But, that only supplies half of what Mojo requires. Statements like these provide no direction for company or employee on how to actually make the product the finest. That is a crucial part of Marketing Mojo.

Here's Callaway Golf's Mojo Formula:

"We make golf equipment that is pleasingly different and demonstrably superior (Core Differentiator) to enhance every type of golfer's enjoyment of the game (Core Benefit)."

With that kind of Mojo Mantra, Callaway Club Designers know the exact litmus test the new products will be put to. Is the product pleasingly different? Is it demonstrably superior? Will it make the game more enjoyable for all types of golfers, pros and amateurs alike?

That's something no mission statement can achieve.

Advanced Mojofication: The Tagline

Taglines are often used in advertisements and after company logos to give an audience a quick sense of what a company does or what the brands stands for. Few taglines are longer than 5 words and even fewer are longer than 7. It's one of the most difficult aspects of Marketing Mojo because it is an immense challenge to condense a company message into just a few words.

Some companies have multiple taglines or switch it from year to year. It is a waste of money and an enemy of Mojofication. If you can't keep a tagline for at least three years, don't even bother having one.

In some instances, your Mantra, or a version of it, may become a company's tagline. Nike's "Just Do It" or Callaway's "A Better Game By Design" are two examples of a Mantra that was transformed into a tagline and managed to motivate employees, vendors, and customers.

While a Mantra should stay relatively unchanged over the years, a tagline may shift slightly over a shorter period of time based on market conditions, product life cycles, etc. (emphasis on slightly). For example, Lexus recently changed its tagline from "The relentless pursuit of perfection" to "The passionate pursuit of perfection." Having a meaningful, memorable, and unique tagline like this can be a powerful marketing tool and can stake serious claim in your industry. But again, it's only a handle, not the Mantra itself.

Let Your Mantra Fly

With your Mojo rolling, and now that you have a pretty good idea of who you are and what you're selling, it is time to get your message out there to motivate employees and others even more. Here's the other half of pillar three: motivation.

Your Mantra is useless unless everyone knows what it is because it transcends marketing. It affects R&D, sales, your physical plant, even how you answer the phones. For example, Callaway Golf's Mantra incorporates the notion of game enjoyment; everything they do reflects that philosophy. When you call Callaway, you can tell immediately when they answer the phone that they pride themselves on your enjoyment.

So, run your Mantra up a flagpole, not to salute it, but to make sure everyone can see it and can understand it. Kick your Mantra off in an all-employee meeting or even a company party. In larger organizations, set it off in a management letter, or even better, a newsletter that provides an explanation. At the very least, post the Mantra on the walls of your physical plant.

Remember to have fun with it. Again, this is not something that should be saluted. Don't be afraid to slap it on t-shirts, put it on balloons, or imprint it on memo pads. The most important thing is that everyone hears the beat and steps to it.

With a unifying direction, it's easier to tackle other marketing problems, since there's no guesswork as to what your company stands for and how people in your organization should act.

6

Jumpstart Your Mantra

By 2007, some $8 billion in television advertising will be skipped by DVR users.

—DigitalEdge.org

A successful marketing campaign is driven by the development of a salient strategy that starts with an exhaustive study of the brand or service, the competition, and the target audience. In other words, great marketing is the result of sound planning.

Strategy is so important that every marketing process should revolve around it. Before producing anything, you should create a "strategic brief" to establish a solid foundation from which to begin. The brief should include establishing clear and reasonable objectives, developing and exploring tactics, and ensuring that the plan is clearer, smarter, more efficient and more focused than your competition.

Developing a Strategic Brief

The strategic brief should be divided into at least seven different, yet interrelated, parts:

1. What are you trying to accomplish?

2. Who are you talking to?

3. What do those people think now?

4. What do you want those people to think?

5. The Nail

6. How does your brand character support this?

7. What ammo do you have?

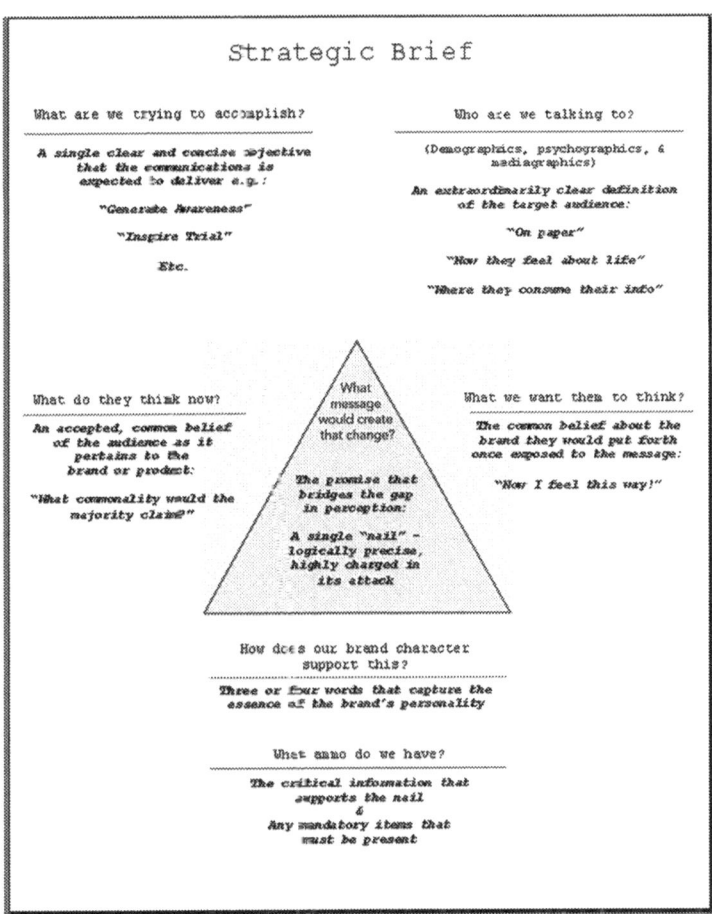

Strategic Brief

What are we trying to accomplish?

A single clear and concise objective that the communications is expected to deliver e.g.:

"Generate Awareness"

"Inspire Trial"

Etc.

Who are we talking to?

(Demographics, psychographics, & mediagraphics)

An extraordinarily clear definition of the target audience:

"On paper"

"How they feel about life"

"Where they consume their info"

What do they think now?

An accepted, common belief of the audience as it pertains to the brand or product:

"What commonality would the majority claim?"

What message would create that change?

The promise that bridges the gap in perception:

A single "nail" – logically precise, highly charged in its attack

What we want them to think?

The common belief about the brand they would put forth once exposed to the message:

"Now I feel this way!"

How does our brand character support this?

Three or four words that capture the essence of the brand's personality

What ammo do we have?

*The critical information that supports the nail
&
Any mandatory items that must be present*

Think of it as a seven step program to developing an in-depth and thorough branding strategy. This process will help jump-start your Mantra. So, give it a shot and develop a marketing strategy for your company's brand. Using this graphic as an example, create your own one-page strategic brief template on which you'll write your responses. It could look like this—but it's best to create a template that makes the most sense to you.

First, what are you trying to accomplish? This is a single, clear, and concise objective that the communications you make are expected to deliver. Not how, but what. For example, you might want to "generate awareness and inspire trial." Write yours down.

Now, who are you talking to? Not just "people who would want to buy my product." This should be an extraordinarily clear definition of your target audience, such as homeowners, 40-55 years old, an annual income of $80,000 or more, and 1-3 children. Today, there is an enormous amount of information about people at your fingertips. Use it!

And, go beyond just the statistics or "demographics." Include how they feel about life, where they find your information, etc. In the age of consumer control, people are more than numbers. They are a collection of aggregate emotions, and these psychographics drive them and their choices. Here's where a little research comes in handy. Studying demographics (i.e., the age, sex, income, and education of a particular population), psychographics (i.e., the attitudes, interests, and opinions of a particular population), and mediagraphics (i.e., the media habits of a particular population) will give you a much clearer view of your target audience and a much more specific idea of who they are and how to reach them. So, who are those people? Write everything you know down.

Next, what do they think now? Just like defining who they are, understanding what your target audience believes is uncovered through research. But, it's a slightly different kind. Rather than statistical analysis, do some field research. It's this simple: talk to your audience. Find out exactly what they think about your industry, your product or your brand. What do they want from it? What do they expect from it? What do they dislike about it? In the end, your goal is to figure out what commonality the majority would claim?

What is the common belief amongst your target audience about your brand or product? Write that down.

Now, what is it that you want them to think? It's number four on the list and a crucial step to creating your strategy. This is the common belief about your brand that you want to create once your audience sees your message. In other words, you want your customers to change their minds from what they think now (Step 3) and instead say, "Now I feel like _____." Or, "Now I believe that _____."

When you have it, write it down.

Now it's time to create the message that's going to change your target audience's perceptions—bridge the gap between what they think now and what you want them to start thinking. It's called the "nail." Sounds difficult right? It is.

Where that moniker comes from might help you better understand it. It's a bit of a morbid metaphor really, but "The Nail" comes from the traveling carnivals of decades ago. Remember the tattooed guy who lies down on a bed of razor-sharp nails and, to the amazement of the audience, comes away with nary a scratch after his 110 lb. assistant dances across his chest? What protected him was the distribution of weight across a thousand points.

In the world of marketing Mojo, that represents a bad strategy. What you should do is eliminate every nail on that bed except one. For the Carnie, that would mean serious injury or death. For your strategic brief, it means focus and a real chance of changing perception.

Advertising agencies and marketers around the world spend millions of dollars every year attempting to create unique messages that will have the potential to make people choose their product over their competitors. Look at Apple, Volvo, and Coors. Their products aren't unique (computers, cars, and beer), but because their messaging is exceptional, so are their businesses.

It's time to get creative. While you don't have to develop a message that mirrors Apple's iPod, you should aspire to create a message that promotes change. It is the promise that bridges the gap in perception that you have illuminated, and it is logically precise and highly charged in its attack.

Think about it and then write it down. (This may be an appropriate time to insert a bookmark and get a pad of scrap paper. Creating "the nail" is very important and no small feat, so don't worry if it doesn't come to you in the midst of reading this book. Ask any creative thinker and they'll tell you that inspiration is more like a bolt of lightning than an on/off button. So, your brand's nail will probably come to you in the middle of the night when you aren't even thinking about it.)

But if you're ready to continue…

With that complete, steps six and seven are a breeze because essentially, you are just restating what you already know. First step six: How does your brand character support your nail? Sound familiar? This is your Core Differentiator: three to five words that capture the essence of your brand's personality and makes your company, your company.

Finally, step seven: What ammo do you have? This is the critical information that supports your nail and makes it true and believable. It also includes any mandatory items that you think must be advertised, such as a 10% promotion, or a Universal Selling Point like the "speed" of the cars being sold. Reference your Core Benefit and write that down.

And with that, you have it. You've just created a strategic brief. If you wrote it in pencil, rewrite it in pen. If it isn't laminated yet, head to Kinko's. This is a platform from which your Mantra will launch. Nonetheless, if you're doing this correctly, the brief is going to light the wick of your brand. The next step is execution. And that begins with effective communication.

7

Alternative Mojo

In 2005, more than 80 million people used instant messaging.

—ClickZ.com

What alternative media sounds like and what it actually means are two very different things. The very definition of alternative (a proposition or situation offering a choice between two or more things, only one of which may be chosen) implies that alternative media is optional. It's not. In fact, alternative media is vital. Many businesses, especially those with a small or no marketing budget which employ alternative media, are able to establish who they are to the business world, their employees, and their customers.

Alternative media means being an ambassador of your own brand—anything you do is a reflection of that brand and everything that comes out of your company is effectively marketing. Everything communicates, pillar four.

The Communications Audit

It begins within your four walls. In your office are a myriad of materials that leave each day with marketing power—letterhead, business cards, fax sheets, memo pads, invoices, company picnic flyers, and PowerPoint® presentations.

Perform a communications audit. Gather all the physical communications pieces you can find, spread them out over a table, and ask yourself, "Do they look like they came from the same company? Do they reflect one brand personality? Or, are they a hodgepodge of pieces thrown together by people in different departments? Do they reflect the type of organization we've decided to become? The audit should reveal a singular, cohesive look and feel to the world outside.

Remember, the size of your marketing budget is inversely proportional to the importance of these pieces. The smaller your budget, the stronger these communication pieces need to be. With no budget, these are your most effective advertising weapons.

The Importance of Design

One of the deadliest marketing mistakes is underestimating the importance of the look and feel of these marketing materials. Whether it's the box your product arrives in, a logo, or a four-color ad, companies often emphasize the content and not the wrapping. Many marketers, unfortunately, think that it doesn't matter what it looks like as long as the message is clear.

But, would you go to an interview in jeans, t-shirt and flip-flops? After all, you are still an intelligent, talented, ambitious person, no matter what you wear. So, why not? One reason: physical presentation has emotional impact on the viewer. It's only human to be attracted to things that are more beautiful, and physical attraction is how interaction and relationships begin. Of course, it's what inside that counts; content seals the deal, but in the beginning, something must provoke interest. Products and companies are no different. Marketing material presented in an accessible, attractive, and simple fashion is essential in Marketing Mojo. Look at the company images Apple and Google have created.

Employees Are Marketers

Fact is, the biggest potential for marketing your company won't cost you a single penny. No one talks more about your company than your staff, and you have the ability to make them ambassadors of your brand. Southwest Airlines is a good example of how employees can change the way a company is viewed by customers—friendly pilots and flight attendants, who actually seem to enjoy their jobs. Their contentment makes it easy for consumers to enjoy traveling.

It can certainly backfire though. You've probably worked for a company you didn't look upon too happily. And when employees don't like the company they work for, ideas, production, and business suffer.

But, more often than not, employees don't want to question a company's direction; they, just as often, don't know what it is. In the end, employees don't want to work for a company that they think is headed in the wrong direction or no direction at all.

Using an informal roundtable discussion or a monthly newsletter, just make sure that your employees know what is going on. As a result, they'll be more content to work for you and become a very powerful alternative marketing tool as a result.

Speaking Engagements

Invest time rather than money. Get involved in your industry through speaking engagements to tell the world about yourself. People are always interested in hearing what other companies are doing, especially when it's interesting.

You don't have to be a maverick in your industry to make a presentation. If you think you don't have anything to talk about, present a problem and a solution. It's more than likely that other people in the industry have had a similar problem and are interested in hearing how to resolve it.

In speaking engagements you have the opportunity to position yourself as an expert. People want to do business with experts.

Write Articles for Online Publications

Becoming a writer has never been easier. The need for original online content continues to grow, even today. With trade sites all over the web, you'll have no problem finding an audience interested in hearing what you have to say. Thousands of websites search out new articles to keep their own sites fresh.

Simply contact the editors of those sites (they'll be glad to hear from you) and let them know that you are interested in submitting articles. Have a couple written to submit with your query, as a sample.

Write a Book

Write a book about the problems you've helped solve within your industry. If the problem solving goes beyond the borders of your industry, that's even better. This will further cement your reputation as an expert, and give you something physical to market. Very few things have the power of a book to motivate a prospect to call you. This will be your most powerful new business tool.

8

Communicating Your Mojo

75% of all Americans use the Internet and spend an average of 3 hours a day online.

—CS.CMU.edu

Have you every heard the cliché, "You are who you hang out with"? Well, your company is who it hangs out with. Or rather, it is defined by the people who make it work.

Again, pillar four, a company's brand is communicated through every aspect. This includes who it is associated with. Nothing communicates more effectively and efficiently than a person. Fact is, getting your Mojo through to the right people will help your business meet more success and endure the ever-fluctuating market it faces.

Reach the Right People

It is necessary to communicate with five primary audiences. (This is in particular order, so best not to shuffle the deck.)

1. Your employees

2. Your current customers

3. Your potential customers

4. Your business partners

5. Investors

Each of these groups plays a crucial role in the success of your company. Each of these groups has its own set of characteristics. And, each of these groups has its own needs. Yet, all of them represent the people you must influence in order to give your company the presence needed to survive and thrive. Without it, you're sunk.

Unfortunately, companies ignore one or more of these groups consistently. These kinds of companies tend to focus on their own upper management as the be-all and end-all audience. They're easy to recognize, too, usually moving in circles, rather than forward.

It is nearly impossible to change strategy without a clear goal in mind. And without a goal, the end result is low employee satisfaction and weak partner relationships. Marketing Mojo represents the opposite of this.

Companies with real Marketing Mojo focus seriously on their employees first. In fact, some Mojofied companies, like Hallmark Cards, hire people for the sole purpose of impacting the corporate culture and making sure the employees understand company goals. They recognize that when their team understands the vision of the company, and its business strategies, it is less expensive than trying to explain it to the end-user of their products. If employees are committed to what the company wants to accomplish, each one of them becomes a "marketeer." Every time they talk to someone about the company, they're selling it. (More on this later.)

> Our first priority should be the people who work for the companies, then the customers, then the shareholders. Because if the staff is motivated, then the customers will be happy, and the shareholders will then benefit through the companies' success.—Richard Branson

Coming in a very close second are current customers. The easiest and least expensive way to earn new business has been and always will be through your current customer relationships. Why? For whatever reason these people have already chosen you.

A great customer relationship isn't very different from a personal one, and friends don't fire friends, so the closer you remain to a customer, the better. Just as in a personal relationship, the more you get to know the customer, the more they will get to know you. And, the more they are likely to share what they know with others.

Amazon.com has nearly mastered the craft of customer relationships. They've become experts at customer retention by communicating valuable information, which customers are actually interested in. On an ongoing basis, they are showing that they care about their customers, and they are doing it without being obtrusive in their lives. Lesson to be learned? Make sure your current customers feel valued by making them a large part of your overall marketing communication objectives.

Now, it is a little pointless to pontificate about the importance of communicating to potential clients. If you don't know this already, then you probably aren't in business. But if you are, then you know that potential customers are the most expensive of all the groups to reach and communicate effectively with. That's why it's important to find the best and least expensive ways to target them.

On to the last group. Gaining the respect of business partners and vendors is vital. They aren't tops on the list, but they're still on it, for two very big reasons:

1. These people talk.

2. You can lower your cost of doing business through them.

Partners and vendors are your direct link to the business community. They have direct links to media avenues that might benefit your company, and they probably know your customers. All these people communicate with each other—for good or ill.

Furthermore, your company is probably partnered with another company. As such, you already know which of them receives better service from you. The ones that you like to work with, the ones that treat you with more respect, and the ones that really understand what you are doing. As a result, they get better value out of you, just like you should be getting better value out of your current partners and vendors.

Preaching the Right Message

What message (if any) is your company sending to the world? Well, it should look and sound a certain way to be most effective.

First of all, you shouldn't be sending "messages." You should be sending "a message." As you read before, no one is waiting in line to listen to you. How could they possibly digest multiple messages from you when it is difficult to assimilate even one? Second, don't tell them about you. Talk about them. Describe how you can make their lives better. That's why you're in business and that's why you'll stay in business. Last, rare is the occasion when the ideas you have to grow your business, match the message that people want to hear. So, mold it. Sculpt it. Shape it. Put your message in context that is relevant. The people that are listening want to hear something good. And they want to hear how you can help them.

Moving at the Right Time

What you've read so far may sound like an organization's "image." But that's only a small part of it. An image, more often than not, is merely a façade. Having Marketing Mojo is getting to the core ideology not only of what a company is, but also what it plans on becoming, and then maintaining that focus.

With Marketing Mojo, you'll clearly define who you are, achieve cohesion in that vision, and then shout it, not just from a mountain top, but a from a strategically positioned mountain top.

So, now that you know who to communicate with, how are you going to do it?

9

Traditional Mojo

Nearly 21% of all media purchases in 2006 are expected to be behavioral targeting purchases.

—iMediaConnection.com

A winning media plan is one that connects with the lifestyle of the target audience. How does it do that? It is action oriented, seeking the most effective mediums. It addresses value, accessing the most cost efficient mediums. It allows for flexibility, utilizing mediums with the broadest reach. And, most of all, it is realistic and measurable.

Often, the absolute number of dollars a company spends in the media marketplace is a measure of strength. Sure, companies that spend millions on media every year can flex their muscles, but in reality, how that money is treated, no matter how much it is, indicates the true strength or weakness of a media plan. Fact is, a winning media plan is built on a solid strategic foundation. That's the difference between being successful and flopping.

This chapter will focus on the Five W's that make up a media plan: **What, Who, Where, When,** and **Weight** and will break Traditional Mojo down into two areas: planning and buying.

So, here's your first W: **What** do you wish to accomplish? What is the overall objective of your media plan? Of course, there can be more than one objective.

For instance, one might be the following: To build brand awareness and inspire trial of Product X by as many women, 18-49 years old, as possible through a specific range of mediums.

Your media plan will affect your target from the moment they know your brand exists—that's brand awareness—until they become loyal customers—that's brand loyalty. At any stage, your media plan should be effective and efficient.

Now, what's your first W? _____
_____
_____
_____
_____
_____

Media Planning

Now, answer these questions:

Who is your message addressed to? This is your target audience.

Where will your advertising take place? This is your target geography, such as a television broadcast area.

When should it be scheduled? This is the seasonality and timing of your advertising.

You know what your goal is, so it's time to figure out who you're talking to, how you're talking to them and when you're going to do it. All this is accomplished with research.

You probably have a general idea of who your target audience is. But for media to be successful, your target needs to be clearly defined. That way you can further determine how to efficiently and effectively reach them.

This is the most important part of your media plan. You should know more about your target audience than they do about themselves; and it must be more than: "People who are interested in purchasing (insert your product or service here)."

Break your audience down using demographics, psychographics, and mediagraphics. Uncover the little nuances that make your target audience your target audience. Uncover what they would call their "daily life," and do it with questions like these:

- Who are these people?

- How old are they?

- Where do they work?

- How much do they work?

- What are their leisure habits?

- How many kids do they have?

- Do they prefer baked or mashed potatoes?

- Do they prefer Bono or Britney?

- When do they wake up and go to sleep?

- Do they write their names in their underwear?

Get inside their minds (without actually exploiting them, which would be intrusive) and dig deep.

Write it all down: _____
_____
_____
_____
_____
_____

Now that you have the "What" and the "Who," it's time for the "Where" and "When." There are some points to consider when you're choosing mediums, besides price per insertion, or cost of placing your ad. Of course, your budget will help dictate where your message goes. But there are ways to circumvent a tight budget and you'll read about those in just a moment. For now, are magazines, TV and radio spots, or the web right for your target audience? Think about this list:

- Audience characteristics (demographics, psychographics, and geography)

- Viewership, readership, listenership patterns and trends

- Program or editorial environment

- Pricing and efficiency

- Duplication with other media

- Positioning opportunities

- Scheduling flexibility

- Merchandising opportunities

- Reproduction opportunity

- Circulation coverage

- Creative options, e.g. magazine inserts

- Showcasing creative

- Financial stability of the vehicle/parent company

- Sales force/trade receptivity

It's a long list. But, by filling all these points into your media plan, your company's marketing will be that much stronger. So, where and when will your advertising take place?

Write that down: _____

_____

_____

_____

_____

_____

Media Buying

Finally, **Weight**. How much media is needed to achieve your objectives? This, for example, is a specific range of magazine, radio, or television ads that you have chosen as your vehicles.

When it comes to purchasing specific media (this is related to the previous three W's), finding unexpected ways to advertise is vital to igniting your media plan and eventually, your brand. For reasons of efficiency and price, purchasing unique vehicles (that's another word for the mediums) is a big differentiator.

It's not as difficult as it sounds. You should place your message with mediums that your target will see and hear as much as possible. This is what people in the Media department call, Reach & Frequency, and it is the foundation of great media. The number of eyes that will see your advertisement is its Reach and the number of times each pair of those eyes will see it is its Frequency. Purchasing mediums intelligently will increase your Reach and Frequency, and consumers who know your brand well are more likely to be transformed into loyal customers.

Of course, choosing a magazine with the highest circulation, or a Super Bowl spot, is not necessarily the best choice. Granted, your message would receive great exposure. But, what good is exposure when it isn't directed at the right eyes or ears? Why market a woman's facial moisturizer during the Super Bowl?

Applying greater frequency against a smaller target is smarter than trying to reach everyone at once. (Not to mention that placing an ad during the Super Bowl might cost you your first born child.) Why be insignificant to everyone when you can be important to someone? That's what you're trying to accomplish—significance. Market that same moisturizer during a Lifetime Movie and you've got some Mojo.

A super effective medium will not only deliver your message to the appropriate eyes, but also widen those eyes a bit. A good example is a recent print campaign for Toshiba Notebooks, where advertisements, targeted at high-income, suburban home owners, were placed in a number of technophile magazines as well as golf and investment magazines. Obviously, it's strategic to place a technological product in technological magazines—you want to read about the latest innovation in laptops, you open *Wired Magazine*. But, how many ads for computers, stereos, etc., are in there? Probably one every few pages—there's that marketing clutter again. So how about reaching the same target audience in a relatively unexpected way? That's right, golf and investment magazines. How many ads for computers, stereos, etc., are in those? Probably one: Toshiba's. That's great media planning, and it stems back to great research.

Your message is only as surprising and bold as the medium in which it is delivered.

You may be saying: "My company isn't Toshiba and we definitely don't have Toshiba's money." Still, no matter what your budget is, you should strive to find highly unique vehicles from which to launch your campaign. It's that kind of thinking that has helped make companies, the Toshiba's and not-Toshiba's, *uber*-successful. Try to find the mediums that resonate effectively with your target. Not only will you reach consumers in an unexpected way, but also you will not waste money. Everyone is the same in that matter: you prefer to get the most bang for your buck. And, why shouldn't you?

Media Mojo in the Age of Consumer Control

As if it weren't hard enough to seek out unique mediums to combat your competition, you have to battle a busier, smarter, and all-powerful consumer. Fortunately, this media philosophy will help you conquer the On-Demand World you advertise in.

As you've read, Mojofying your media plan means selecting unique mediums to reach a target consumer. That means more and more research into your target audience. And, in an On-Demand world, that means knowing, out of the hundreds of channels available to watch, which shows they prefer. That means finding out, from the millions of websites they might visit, the sites they frequent the most. Most of all, that means connecting with the consumer on a personal level. Emails, interactive product demos, promotion updates, etc. You want consumers to be loyal? Offer your product or service in a personal way.

While media fragmentation has given consumers more options and more power, you in turn have the ability, more so than ever before, to research and collect data about your customers and prospects, to understand them, and to know them. It's not as difficult as it seems. With so much innovation, meeting these people on a personal level is much less time consuming than it ever was. Actually making contact takes as much as time as writing an email and pushing SEND—not too long.

Advertisers must take advantage of consumer control. Amidst this growth in power, consumers are, in fact, telling you exactly what they want and when they want it. The shows they watch, the websites they visit and the products and services they want to buy. This wealth of information is available to you, and getting your hands on it can turn the world of On-Demand into a land of opportunity.

10

New Media Mojo

Since 2000, magazine circulation has declined by nearly 20 million.

—Magazine.org

One of the biggest contributors to media fragmentation is the rise of new communication technologies. Consumers' media habits are constantly changing as they spend increasing amounts of time on the Internet, using their cell phones, and using products like the digital video recorder to record their favorite shows.

In the last ten years, marketers have responded with a variety of activities to engage the consumer. You probably have heard of (or are currently doing) most of them: online marketing, wireless advertising, viral (Word-of-Mouth) marketing, sponsoring consumer-generated media (i.e. blogs), etc.

You won't read about everything you need-to-know about new marketing techniques in this chapter. In fact, you'll barely scratch the surface of these activities. But, this chapter will help you begin to infuse Mojo into your new media advertising. (Truly discussing the topic of "New Media Mojo" would require an entirely dedicated book. Not a bad idea, now that I think about it.)

Online

Whether you are engaging in rich media banners, behavioral targeting, search optimization, paid search advertising, affiliate marketing, email marketing, podcasting, RSS feeds, building and managing complex data driven websites, or any other online initiative, you have undoubtedly figured out that the Internet is an incredibly efficient direct marketing vehicle. Technology developed in the last several years has enabled marketers to track online campaign results in near real-time. You can rotate your creative or change your bid strategy (paid search) literally within minutes of assessing the campaign's conversion effectiveness, based on the cost-per-sale or cost-per-lead of a specific creative execution.

Still, the Internet is the most undervalued medium (due in part to the reaction to the 2001 dot-bust) there is still a tremendous amount of ad inventory unsold. At the time of writing this, the Internet represents 15% of consumer's media consumption; however, it accounts for only 3-4% of total ad spending.

Whether branding or selling, how do you take advantage of this opportunity and infuse Mojo into your online marketing?

Develop a Message Map: Create a list of agreed-upon and pre-approved marketing messages that you and your agency, if you have one, can use for testing creative (e.g., copy points and images). A terrific example—and an illustration of how to find a happy medium between corporate positioning and communicating with consumers on their terms—is Oakley's paid search creative test.

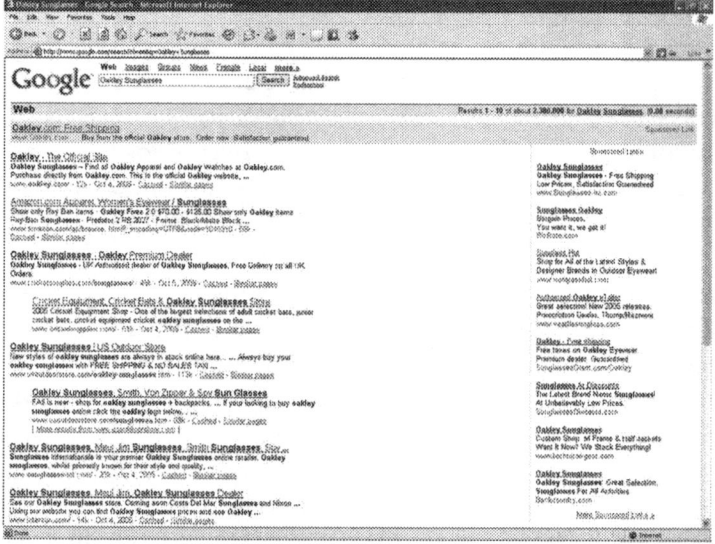

These copy points were used in a test on Google Adwords. The goal was to determine the combination of a header & a descriptor that most cost effectively generated sales of sunglasses (on Oakley.com). Here is the test matrix:

Example: Keyword = Oakley Sunglasses

Test	Headline	Description Line 1	Description Line 2
A	Oakley Sunglasses	One year warranty and free shipping.	Satisfaction guaranteed. Order now!
B	Oakley Sunglasses	Buy direct and get free shipping.	Shop now! Satisfaction guaranteed.
C	Oakley.com: Free Shipping	Buy from the official Oakley store.	Order now. Satisfaction guaranteed.
D	Eyewear by Oakley	Free shipping on Oakley sunglasses.	Direct from the source!

While the differences between these example cells may seem subtle, there was a statistically significant difference in the response—in fact there was a 75% variance in the click-to-purchase ratio between the lowest converting and highest converting combination of headline/descriptions. In this case, Oakley was able to use the pre-approved copy, with the help of the Google test, to describe the product in a way that was most compelling to consumers.

Engage Users with Interactivity: Instead of posting a static image of your latest product(s) on your website, develop interactive product demos or tutorials.

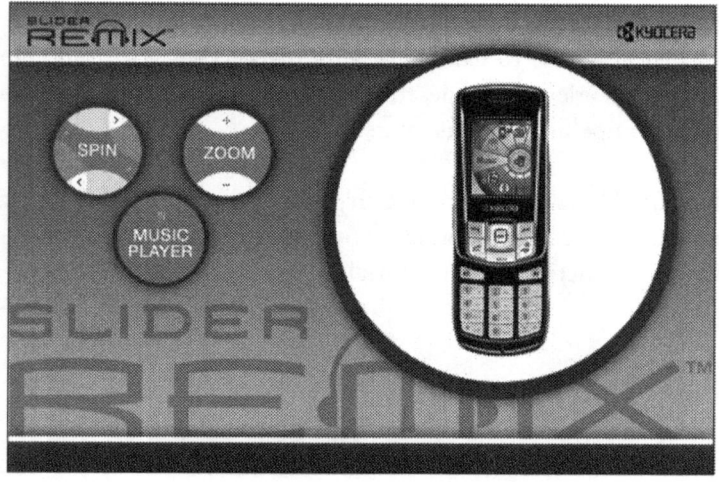

You can also create 3-D renderings of your products so that visitors can virtually experience them. Rendering enables users to interact with a product by spinning it around, looking at it from all sides, opening it, closing it, etc.

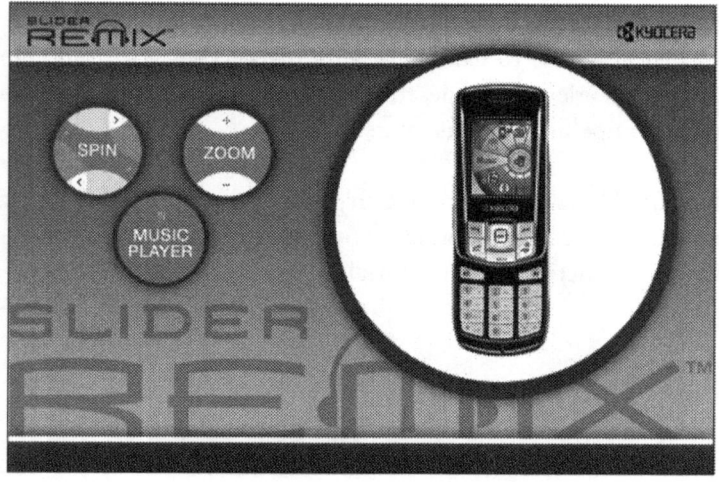

Personalize the User Experience: Develop a dynamic (i.e., database driven) website so that users can set certain preferences for their return visits. Or, you can cookie them to provide relevant information upon their return visits. And, if you have a large website, you should provide users with the option to search your site for content and/or products.

Become a Publisher: Leverage your subject matter expertise (every company is an authority on something) and make it available to consumers in an objective way (don't sell, educate). A great example is the "IQ" section on Openwave's website. The IQ section provides visitors with information, articles, white papers, and press releases on their subject matter expertise: software solutions for Carriers (wireless data products) and Broadband Operators (email products).

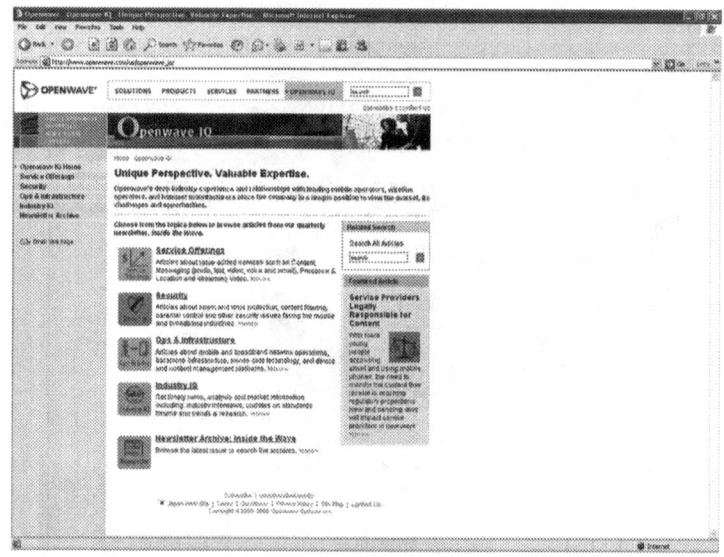

Why go to the effort of becoming a publisher? In addition to being a great use of the medium, marketers can exchange content for customer data, which can be used for lead generation (B2B enterprise sales) and retention (B2C) efforts. The content you publish can also be used in your public relations efforts, generating awareness of your business. And, if done properly, it establishes you as a credible expert and leader in your category.

Mine and Analyze Your Data: Mojofied companies understand that by sifting through the myriad of data points available to them, they will find insights that can fundamentally change their business.

There are only two types of data points: interaction and dialog.

1. Interaction data points measure activity on your site and are typically tracked to a specific action or "goal" page. Typical actions include sales, leads, referrals (commonly known as "forward-to-a-friend"), and subscriptions (data capture).

2. Dialog data points can be tracked to existing customers or prospects for which you have a historical record. Whether you have communicated with them via email marketing, or they have established a membership at your site, your goal is to retain them and turn them into loyal advocates of your company/brand.

Site	Impressions	Clicks	CTR	Dealer Searches	Newsletter Signup	Lead Forms	CBL	Total Prospects	CTL	Ad Costs	CPC / Visitor	CPP
	15,737	2,020	12.7%	467		0	41	518	25.6%	$660.59	$0.33	$1.28
	N/A	2,331	N/A	65		5	102	190	8.2%	$1,311.39	$0.56	$6.90
	N/A	35	N/A	1		2	2	5	14.3%	N/A	N/A	N/A
	8,705	54	0.0%	11		0	15	26	48.1%	N/A	N/A	N/A
	N/A	1	N/A	6		0	4	10	1000.0%	N/A	N/A	N/A
	30,577	3	0.0%	6		0	0	8	0.0%	N/A	N/A	N/A
	64,733	7	0.0%	8		0	0	8	0.0%	N/A	N/A	N/A
	730,495	2,314	0.3%	37		0	29	66	2.9%	$2,156.66	$0.93	$32.68
	593,680	1,802	0.3%	8		2	8	72	4.0%	$1,414.00	$0.78	$19.64
All Sites	1,443,573	8,547	0.6%	567	N/A	17	201	895	10.4%	$7,135.71	$0.83	$8.95

Site	Impressions	Clicks	CTR	Dealer Searches	Newsletter Signup	Lead Forms	CBL	Total Prospects	CTL	Ad Costs	CPC / Visitor	CPP
	N/A	8,622	N/A	2,818		41	181	2,841	33.3%	$4,122.35	$0.48	$1.45
	N/A	13,776	N/A	334		41	176	551	4.0%	$8,248.35	$0.60	$14.97
	N/A	238	N/A	22		86	8	170	60.3%	N/A	N/A	N/A
	10,688	76	0.7%	11		0	15	26	34.2%	N/A	N/A	N/A
	N/A	189	N/A	6		55	0	70	37.0%	$3,176.48	$16.81	$45.36
	30,577	3	0.0%	5		0	0	5	0.0%	$0.00	$0.00	$0.00
	64,733	7	0.0%	6		0	0	6	0.0%	$0.00	$0.00	$0.00
	3,369,205	14,164	0.4%	247		6	81	328	2.3%	$14,303.39	$1.01	$43.61
	2,409,246	7,293	0.3%	186		8	46	253	3.5%	$6,503.00	$0.89	$25.70
All Sites	5,833,619	46,353	0.7%	3,473	N/A	333	657	5,235	2.7%	$37,613.57	$1.20	$6.73

But, being online is only a part, albeit a significant part, of Mojofying your company. Here are two more excellent examples of new media that can help mojofy your business.

Wireless

As of January 2005, there are nearly 170,000,000 wireless subscribers in the United States and that number continues to grow at an exponential rate. Those subscribers fill cyberspace with about 2.5 billion text messages each month; more than 80,000,000 a day! (mmaglobal.com) That's not just a lot of chatter. That's a vast amount of time that people spend with their personal wireless communicators—cell phones, pagers, wired PDAs, and others.

Marketers who want to communicate with the very consumers they spend millions of dollars chasing, can now take advantage of this unique and extremely personal medium in which to do it. Needless to say, reaching a customer in this fashion means toeing a thin line that separates spam advertising and "personalized marketing." But, if you can create a welcomed dialogue with your customers through their wireless devices, you've just accessed an inexpensive and highly effective, one-to-one medium.

With double digit growth in the wireless communication industry, mobile campaigns should be an integral part of your marketing mix. Leveraging mobile marketing as soon as possible can mean improving the ROI of your total marketing budget.

Remember: consumers are intelligent and, worse, they're powerful. Mobile marketing is unique because it's personal, but that just means consumers can tune you out with a thumb-click. The goal is to earn their trust by answering the ever-present question: what can you do for me? So, begin by offering incentives like coupons for a free beverage or free ring tones; and wrap in better creative. Make sure the consumer feels valued and that you are stimulating an ongoing dialogue. Retaining interest means increasing ROI on a long term basis.

Word-of-Mouth

How do you motivate consumers to provide information about you and your brand to other consumers? Simple. Give them a reason to talk and provide a specific environment in which to do it. Believe it or not, if you provide it, they will come.

The phenomenon of Word-of-Mouth marketing is something that most marketers are only now beginning to utilize. To do it effectively, you must build active and mutually beneficial consumer-to-consumer and consumer-to-marketer communications (all, of course, within your marketing objective). Encourage it by listening closely to your consumers, by making it easy for them to tell their friends, and by ensuring that influential individuals, such as politicians and pop stars, are aware of your brand's great qualities.

According to WOMMA, the Word-of-Mouth Marketing Association, the five steps to effective Word-of-Mouth marketing are:

1. Educating your consumers with valuable content about your brand/product/service.

2. Identifying the people who will most likely express their opinion about it.

3. Making it easy to share information with others and your company.

4. Measuring the results of those responses that you collect.

5. Responding to those results by reshaping your brand/product/service.

So, how do you infuse this kind of marketing into your business? Well, here are some of WOMMA's examples of Word of Mouth:

- **Viral:** Creating entertaining messages designed to be passed along by email.

- **Blogs:** Sharing information in a pseudo-dialogue fashion, much like an online bulletin.

- **Referrals:** Allowing satisfied customers to refer their friends with the tools you provide.

- **Seeding:** Placing the right product in the right hands at the right time.

- **Influencer:** Identifying key groups who will influence the opinions of others.

Involving your customers means allowing them to directly impact you and your brand/product/service. Whether you create a viral campaign or a company blog, engage them to find out how you can sell better. Be sure to make it personal and give your customer a voice. In the end, they'll have a product that meets their needs. And, you'll have a hot product.

11

Measuring Your Mojo

> In 1995 there were 1.3 million web pages available commercially. By 2000, there were 1 billion.
>
> —*InsidePolitics.org*

Measurement and Analytics

Measurement and Analytics is about collecting pertinent information to track the sales you don't make. It's relatively easy to record how many people bought your product. But what about the people who saw your ad, read it, but didn't buy your product? What about the people who saw your promotion but didn't even read it? Collecting information about these people can help you with future campaign strategy.

As with any scientific data collection, this information is used to test and apply knowledge for the future to help produce desired outcomes; in your case, decrease costs and increase revenue.

Don't think of the strategic process as a timeline. Think of it more as a circle. It is ongoing and never ending. Measurement and Analytics keeps you trucking around that circle.

While the best tracking is done online, there are ways to track an offline campaign, albeit more cumbersome; for instance, using a toll-free number, a brochure order form, coupons, promotional codes, an event registration, a consumer survey, etc.

Of course, the best way to track any offline campaign is with online support. In this case, your advertising campaign, print, billboard, or otherwise, includes a mention of your website. Using this tactic allows you to track the reach and effectiveness of your offline campaign. However, since most people you are reaching with a billboard or print ad may not necessarily use the Internet to research, shop, or purchase what you're selling them, it can be slightly less effective.

However, by developing a media plan that includes interactive marketing or is completely interactive, you not only take advantage of a less expensive and more versatile method of advertising, but you also open the door to an extremely effective method of tracking your campaign.

Online Tracking

First, set goals for your site. In other words, establish which page or pages you want users to visit on your website. These are your Goal Pages.

Here is an example: When consumers visit your site, you want them to fill out a lead form. The Goal Page, in this case, would be the "Thank you for filling out the form" page or any other page that follows the submission of their information. The lead form page shouldn't be your goal because it doesn't necessarily mean that users have filled it out. The "Thank You" page ensures that they have.

Write your Goal Page down:_____

_____

_____

_____

_____

_____

Web Analytics

Simply put, Web Analytics is the process by which one studies every component of a site and the traffic it receives. There's a wealth of information hiding in your site's log files, which are the records of every action taken by every visitor on a given site. These can tell you how many people came to a page; how they found the site; if they used a search engine like Google and what keywords they entered; how many items (images, etc.) displayed on any given page to each and every visitor; and much more.

The most important thing to remember in Web Analytics is to look at your site as a whole. Pay less attention to minute details, if for no other reason than the overabundance of data. The inundation of details alone, in your reports, could drive you insane.

The Internet provides a user with nearly infinite paths in and out of your site and Web Analytics tools collect data and report on each of those sessions (a fancy word for visit) no matter how long or what type. It would be easy to look at these reports and wonder why a user only spent three seconds on your site or why they spent an hour on your site when the average session is only two minutes. Focusing on such details often proves to be counterproductive.

What should you look for? Aggregates and trends. You created your website for qualified traffic—more page views, longer user sessions, and a higher rate of return users, among other things.

How do you look for it? Web Analytics reports. Run them at least once a month. Monthly reports will give you sufficient data to base your marketing decisions on without letting too much time pass between those developments. Day-to-day and weekly reports don't provide enough information and you may see wild fluctuations in session data. And, reports spanning longer than a month may provide a better skew of data, but that's too long to wait to make needed improvements.

Web Analytics Reports

Referrals: Essentially, this report is a look at where your users have been on the Web and what types of sites they associate with yours. It will show the last site a user visited before clicking through to your site. These are extremely useful in developing online media plans through advertising opportunities and finding potential business affiliates.

Search Terms: This report will show what terms users enter into search engines like Google, Yahoo, MSN, etc. to find your site (this does not include paid search advertisements). Obviously, this helps determine the value of your paid search terms, but maybe just as important is the ability to better understand the vernacular of your target audience. It is common for marketers to become too familiar with the jargon of their business and forget their customers may use completely different verbiage. For example, a telecommunications company should not have the word "telecommunications" anywhere in their content or search efforts because most people simply call it a "phone company."

Top Exit Pages: This report should be used to identify key pages of a site that users may have a hard time with to improve usability. This may be a form page or a check out process page but most commonly is the home page.

Visitors: Look for a steady increase in overall average monthly visitors.

Unique vs. Returning Visitors: You'll naturally want to look for improvements in this report, often shown as a ratio, over longer periods of time because several factors can have an effect on the bottom line each month. For example, the percentage of returning visitors can appear deceivingly low, if there is a sudden influx of unique visitors (perhaps from other marketing efforts). A gradual increase of the percentage of returning visitors is a good indication that people find your site useful and may even recommend it to others.

Page views: Also, look for overall increases in page views and the average page views per session. This is an indication of how well your site engages users, or how "sticky" it is. Decreases in page views often indicate a lack of interest in a site's content. However, account for large influxes of traffic, which can mean a decrease in page views. In this case, the site isn't becoming less interesting to the normal flow of users; it's receiving new, less qualified traffic.

Average User Session Length: Study the average amount of time users spend on your site as an aggregate. Doing otherwise may mean that the data has a much more profound impact on the overall outcome than it should. Consider users leaving their computer unattended for long periods of time while still on your site. This could push the average session length way up. On the other hand, consider if your site doesn't load properly, users will leave much faster. This can pull an average way down.

Web Analytics in a Nutshell

1. Scrutinize them. There are a number of issues outside of your control that hinder the accuracy of these numbers.

2. Use common sense. Real analysis means considering the big picture, including marketing efforts, newness of the campaign, usability, and other extraneous circumstances. Look at these reports individually and in relation to one another as all of the information is related.

Campaign Tracking

All Web Analytics tools should have a campaign tracking component that allows you to flag and highlight specific traffic as there is no way to distinguish it in log files. This type of functionality enables advertisers to tag links and advertisements with a unique URL, which contains parameters identifying each part of every campaign. Those parameters are read by the JavaScript on the site and duplicated in campaign reports.

Most tools that have a campaign tracking component also have a campaign-tracking URL "builder," which simply asks for several pieces of information be added to the URL and hierarchically displays them in campaign reports.

For example:

- A root URL (landing page)—e.g., http://www. yoursite.com/events

- The marketing effort—e.g., media

- The site—e.g., Yahoo

- The area of the site—e.g., news

- A unique identifier—e.g., top banner

Using these examples, the tool would then generate a URL for that campaign, and would look like this in the address bar:

> http://www.yoursite.com/events/
> ?Effort_id=media&Site_id=yahoo&
> Placement_id=news&Name_id=top_banner

In this example URL, each parameter would speak to the JavaScript on that page and essentially flag the user as the one who came from the "top banner," in the "news" section, of the

"Yahoo" campaign, in the overall online "media" campaign portfolio. Then, this information would be displayed in campaign reports and you could simply identify which campaigns are producing more conversions and/or sales. This process is called "campaign optimization."

12

Mojo in Action

Radio listenership is at a 27-year low.
—FutureofMusic.org

Marketing Mojo is a powerful formula. It puts a business on steroids.

Starbuck's can flex—they turned drinking coffee into a trend. Target can too—they brought K-Mart to its knees. And, of course, there's Nike, which has the biggest muscles of them all. They just flash the Swoosh and consumers line up at shoe retailers everywhere to get the latest pair of Air Jordan's or Air Force Ones. This is Mojo at its finest.

But these marketing giants aren't the only companies that can reap the benefits. Again, it isn't about the size of a marketing budget; it's whether you use those dollars effectively. There are dozens of smaller companies that have their business clicking on all cylinders. Like Nike, they managed to make every dollar they spent work like five and, as a result, will be in business for a long time.

But the proof is in the success. And here's the proof...

Introducing Toshiba Notebooks

Toshiba Notebooks is undeniable proof that Marketing Mojo works. They had the challenge of marketing a state-of-the-art convergence laptop that featured all the functionality of a regular computer coupled with a TV tuner, DVD player, and DVR. It's called the Qosmio.

At the time of its introduction, the idea of digital convergence was relatively foreign to consumers and that posed a challenge. How does Toshiba introduce the Qosmio as a new category notebook, when consumers had just recently grown accustomed to typical notebooks? (It was only in June, 2005 that laptops had finally begun outselling desktops—*yahoo.com*.)

Here's the end of the story: Toshiba's Notebook Division met their quarterly sales goals both online and in retail outlets. As a result of that success, Qosmio would continue to be positioned as the leading product in the notebook-convergence category.

So how did they move beyond the challenge to the success? They popped a bottle of Marketing Mojo.

Solutions Begin With Strategy

It began with an in-depth strategic brief.

How would this convergence product exist in the minds of the consumers? Should it be marketed as a computer wrapped in all the bells and whistles or all the bells and whistles wrapped in a computer?

Answering this question meant identifying the target audience: the "modern household," which was composed of the "prosumer," the "gatekeeper," and the "influencer." (These are all just fancy words for the father, mother, and child.) The prosumer was someone who wanted to add the Qosmio to his growing list of digital toys. The gatekeeper wanted to justify the purchase and ensure that adding it to the home would compliment the current décor and overall feel. Finally, the influencer, one or more, wanted a fun, entertaining product that he, she, or they could show-off to friends.

It meant the Qosmio would best serve the modern household as an entertainment system before a business tool and should be marketed as a "4-in-1 entertainment center to go." Marketing pieces would feature lifestyle versus features and benefits, media would be retail focused, and promotions would be content related.

With all that in mind, Toshiba identified the target audience even further. Through exhaustive research they would market the Qosmio to:

- Married adults with children

- Primarily 35-54 years old

- Own a home

- Income of $100,000+

- Affinity for new technology

- College graduates–

- Suburban

- 1-3 children

- 3-5+ total within household

And the brief was born:

What were they trying to accomplish? Communicate Toshiba's leadership position.

Who were they talking to? *Demographic*: the modern household. *Psychographic*: mobile, techno-savvy. *Mediagraphic*: Heavy Internet users, heavy readers.

What did they think then? I am skeptical about convergence entertainment products.

What did they want them to think? Qosmio is a high-quality and compact entertainment system.

What message would create that change? Radical digital media to go.

How did Toshiba's brand character support that? Ingenious.

What ammo did they have? Qosmio offers state-of-the-art convergence; i.e., 4-in-1.

Great Marketing Requires Great Media

There was the launching pad. It was time to light the fuse.

The media plan developed from the strategic brief called for the following:

- Magazine and newspaper print ads

- Online banner ads

- Paid search advertising on sites such as Google.com

- Online promotions

- In-store displays

- Holiday catalogs

- A microsite featuring a 3D product tour and viral marketing opportunities through Q-Cards (an interactive e-card)

It would all have the same look and feel, as well. The common theme throughout the print campaigns, the web, POP, and promotions was to include consistent lifestyle imagery, functionality icons referring to the Qosmio's 4-in-1 controls, bright product shots, and copy describing the benefits of convergence technology, such as "Take your fun wherever life takes you." The campaign was designed to push the boundaries of creativity but still follow the established strategy closely.

Here's an example of a print ad for Qosmio:

Here's another example, this time of the website:

These are the point-of-purchase promotions:

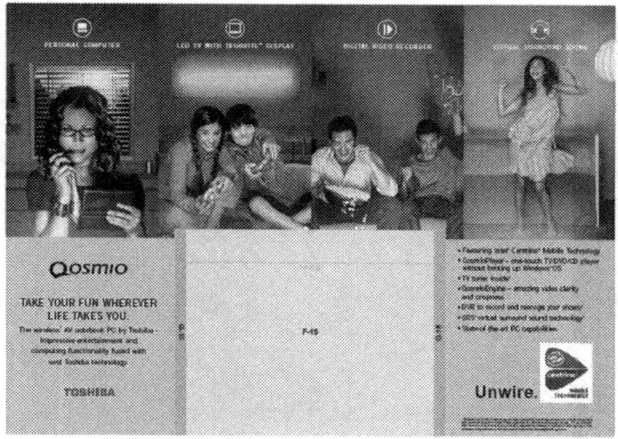

And, finally, the online banners:

Great Results Are Not Optional

The Mojo worked.

Was there ever any question?

Using detailed measurement and analytics we measured the effectiveness of the marketing efforts by tracking response to online banners and promotions, partner URL activity, and microsite activity. There were millions of banner impressions, they sent millions of opt-in emails, and engaged hundreds of thousands of unique visitors on their microsite.

By identifying and understanding the target, developing a sound strategy, choosing media wisely and portraying the right image, Toshiba managed to make every dollar they spent work like five and in doing so, grow their bottom line. Today, Toshiba Notebooks stands on a pedestal in the world of notebooks and digital convergence. They've managed to achieve and maintain a high level of success in the unforgiving market of consumer technology.

13

A Mojo Roadmap

Between 2004 and 2010, the use of podcasting among US consumers will enjoy a compound annual growth rate (CAGR) of 101%.

—MacMinute.com

A Mojo Checklist

Up to this point, you've read what needs to be done to jumpstart your company/brand. The Mojo Roadmap is the summation.

Treat the Mojo Roadmap like a checklist. (Isn't checking off a completed task on a "to-do" list is one of those small pleasures that makes life grand?) The real beauty of this list, though, is that if followed correctly, after the last checkmark and with enough Mojo, your business will be booming—excuse the cliché.

	Define your company and what services it provides
	List Core Values
	Create Core Differentiator
	Create Core Benefit
	Create your Mojo Mantra
	Place your old Mission Statement in storage closet
	Create a company tagline
	Let your Mantra fly (i.e., tell everyone)
	Create a strategic brief
	Rest and stretch (Optional)
	Perform internal communications audit
	Coordinate and redesign company assets
	Enhance communication lines within your company
	Communicate through the appropriate mediums
	Get your company online
	Optimize your campaigns
	Utilize measurement and analytics for tracking
	Schedule speaking engagements
	Write online publications
	Write a book
	Bask in your success (optional, but highly recommended)

Index

978-0-595-37642-1
0-595-37642-8